W9-AVT-042

Frederick Douglass

History Maker Bios

Catherine A. Welch

LERNER PUBLICATIONS COMPANY • MINNEAPOLIS

For Eileen

The author thanks Mary Ellen Delaney, Colleen Rowe, and the staff of the Monroe, CT, Public Library for help in gathering material for this book.

Illustrations by Tim Parlin

Lerner Publications Company
A division of Lerner Publishing Group
241 First Avenue North
Minneapolis, MN 55401 U.S.A.

Website address: www.lernerbooks.com

Library of Congress Cataloging-in-Publication Data

Welch, Catherine A.
     Frederick Douglass / by Catherine A. Welch.
        p.   cm. — (History maker bios)
     Summary: A biography of the man who, after escaping slavery, became an orator, writer, and leader in the abolitionist movement in the nineteenth century.
     Includes bibliographical references and index.
     ISBN-13: 978–0–8225–4672–6 (lib. bdg. : alk. paper)
     ISBN-10: 0–8225–4672–8 (lib. bdg. : alk. paper)
     1. Douglass, Frederick, 1817?–1895—Juvenile literature. 2. African American abolitionists—Biography—Juvenile literature. 3. Abolitionists—United States—Biography—Juvenile literature. 4. Antislavery movements—United States—History—19th century—Juvenile literature. [1. Douglass, Frederick, 1817?–1895. 2. Abolitionists. 3. African Americans—Biography.] I. Title.
     E449.D75 W46 2003
     973.8'092—dc21   2002006840

Manufactured in the United States of America
2 3 4 5 6 7 – JR – 11 10 09 08 07 06

TABLE OF CONTENTS

INTRODUCTION

Before the Civil War, four million African Americans were slaves. Frederick Douglass was born a slave. But he had the spirit of a freeman. He had the courage to lead others to freedom.

He escaped from his slave master, and he worked to end slavery. He wrote thousands of articles and letters, and gave over two thousand speeches. His words had the power to change people's minds. Frederick Douglass was a hero to African Americans and became one of America's greatest leaders.

This is his story.

1 THE HORRORS OF SLAVERY

As a child, Frederick wanted to know his birthday. White children knew their birthdays. But white masters did not want slaves to know their birthdays. Many masters did not even want slaves to live as families. Frederick's mother was a slave named Harriet Bailey. His father was a white man— maybe Harriet's master.

Frederick's birth in February 1818 was listed with the births of other slave children.

Frederick Augustus Washington Bailey was born in February 1818, in Maryland. When he was an infant, "Old Master" sent him to stay with Harriet's parents. Old Master forced Harriet to work in the fields, twelve miles away.

Grandmamma Betsy was kind to Frederick and the other grandchildren in her care. She let Frederick run wild and free in the sunshine and fresh air near Tuckahoe Creek.

Grandmamma's cabin was simple, with a clay floor and no windows. But it kept the children safe from the winter's frost. And Frederick felt safe and loved.

Frederick lived in a slave cabin like this.

One day he learned that the cabin belonged to Old Master. Then he learned that Grandmamma and all the children belonged to Old Master.

Frederick was six when a sad-looking Grandmamma took him on a hike. Frederick did not know where they were going. He clung to Grandmamma's skirts.

Grandmamma brought Frederick to Wye House, on Colonel Lloyd's plantation. Old Master worked for Colonel Lloyd.

That day, Frederick met his brother Perry and sisters, Sarah and Eliza. While Frederick was busy meeting them, Grandmamma slipped away. That night, Frederick cried himself to sleep.

The next days, Frederick explored the plantation. He was sad but curious. There were houses, barns, stables, and blacksmith shops. Nearby was a windmill. A large sailing ship was docked at the river's edge.

The white owner of the plantation and his family lived in the large, white Great House. They feasted on roast turkey, ducks, melons, and wine.

SLAVE CHILDREN

Slave children on the Lloyd plantation were poorly clothed. Young children, up to age ten, did not usually work in the fields. So the slaveholders did not give them shoes, stockings, jackets, or trousers. The children got only two coarse shirts each year.

Sometimes the old slaves shared their cornmeal and sour milk with Frederick.

The slaves ate spoiled meat and coarse cornmeal. Frederick and the other children used oyster shells to scoop their cornmeal mush from a tray. The tray was set on the kitchen floor or on the ground outside. Many times Frederick had to fight with the dog for crumbs.

Frederick played with the other children. He tried to make the best of his new life. At night he slept in a closet near the kitchen. When it was cold, he slid into an empty grain sack to keep warm.

Frederick watched the slave men and women work in the fields in rain and scorching heat. He heard their sad songs.

One morning he was awakened by cries and shrieks. He peeked through the cracks of his closet boards. He saw his young Aunt Esther and Old Master.

CRACK! Old Master's whip lashed across her back. Esther screamed. "Have mercy," she cried. But Old Master did not have mercy. He whipped her again and again and again.

Frederick stayed huddled in the closet— shocked, angry, and silent. If he said or did anything, he might be whipped next.

Masters could whip their slaves for any offense, large or small.

2 THE DREAM OF FREEDOM

One day when Frederick was eight, he was told to scrub himself clean in the creek. He was given his first pair of pants. Then he was sent to Baltimore to the home of a white man named Hugh Auld.

Hugh's wife, Sophia, greeted Frederick with kind eyes and a smile. Frederick's job was to run errands and take care of Hugh and Sophia's two-year-old son, Tommy.

Frederick soon learned that city slaves were better fed and clothed than plantation slaves. He was allowed to sleep in a real straw bed with a real blanket.

Sophia Auld had never been a slaveholder. She treated Frederick like he belonged in her family. He and Tommy listened to her read the Bible and sing hymns. Frederick felt like a child again.

Sophia Auld taught Frederick to read.

One day, Sophia boasted to her husband that she was teaching Frederick to read. Hugh exploded with rage. He ordered her to stop. He warned her about the dangers of letting a slave read and learn. A slave with knowledge would run away!

Sophia's gentle voice and smile disappeared. The teaching stopped. But Frederick learned to spell from the white boys he met on the streets of Baltimore. Sometimes, he talked to them about slavery. They told Frederick he had the right to be free. But Frederick thought he would be a slave forever.

Frederick ran errands on the streets and docks of Baltimore, shown here from across the harbor in 1830.

From the time he was a young boy, Frederick heard about slaves running away.

When he was about thirteen, he bought a book, *The Columbian Orator.* He had earned the money for it by shining boots. Some of the speeches in the book were about freedom. Frederick hid by the docks and practiced the speeches. He learned to speak with strong words and passion.

Frederick listened when people talked about slavery. He learned of slaves running away. He learned of slaves setting fire to barns and killing their white masters. He learned about people called abolitionists. They wanted to end slavery. This gave Frederick hope.

Prayer meetings also lifted Frederick's spirits. He prayed with other blacks. They believed God would free them.

When Frederick was fifteen, he was sent to the country house of Thomas Auld, Hugh's brother. Frederick almost starved there. He had to steal food to survive. Life was harder, but the dream of freedom stayed alive. He started a Sunday school for black children. But Master Thomas quickly learned of the school and stopped the teaching. He tried to whip the hope of freedom out of Frederick. When he failed, he sent Frederick to Edward Covey, who loved whipping slaves.

Frederick was often whipped by Edward Covey. Frederick wondered, "Why am I a slave? Why are some people slaves, and others masters?"

Masters often hired out their slaves to work in other farmers' fields.

Covey made Frederick work long hours in the field—in burning heat, freezing cold, rain, and snow. On Sundays, Frederick was bone tired and sore from whippings. He no longer dreamed of freedom.

One day, Frederick decided he wouldn't be whipped anymore. He was six feet tall. He had grown strong and powerful. He battled with Covey for two hours and won. Covey never whipped him again.

The next year, Frederick worked on William Freeland's farm. There, Frederick got enough food and enough time to eat it. But he was still a slave. Once again, he dreamed of freedom.

On Sundays he led a secret school for his fellow slaves. He talked about escaping north, to the free states, where there was no slavery. But how far away were these states? Even if he could find his way there, reaching a free state would not make him a freeman. He could be caught and returned to his slave owner.

Still, the chance of freedom was worth the risk. Frederick and five other slaves planned to escape. They could find their way by following the North Star. But before they could escape, the masters heard of their plan.

Frederick and his friends planned to escape up the Chesapeake Bay to a free state in the North.

Frederick was taken to jail for trying to run away. This drawing is from Frederick's autobiography.

Frederick was dragged to jail. The slave masters questioned him. They decided Frederick was a troublemaker. He was sure to plan another escape. So Frederick was sent back to Hugh Auld in Baltimore.

Hugh sent Frederick to work for a shipbuilder. Frederick became an expert in using caulker's tools. He patched cracks in ships. Even though Frederick did the work, he had to give Hugh his wages. Sometimes he was allowed to keep a litle money.

FREED SLAVES

After the Revolutionary War, the idea of "freedom for all" spread slowly in the United States. Some masters believed that "all men are created equal." They freed their slaves. Other masters freed only their favorite slaves. Some slaves bought their own freedom. And children born to freed slaves were born free. Anna Murray's parents were freed before her birth.

Frederick met many free blacks who could read and write. And he met Anna Murray, a free black woman. Anna worked as a housekeeper. They soon grew fond of each other and wanted to get married. But Frederick was afraid he would be sold to a new master in the Deep South. So he and Anna saved their money and planned Frederick's escape.

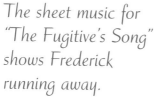
The sheet music for "The Fugitive's Song" shows Frederick running away.

One day twenty-year-old Frederick dressed himself as a sailor. He hopped onto a train as it left the station and paid his fare to the conductor.

The time on the train seemed endless. Frederick's heart pounded in his chest. He worried that he would see someone who knew him. When the train arrived in the next town, Frederick got on a boat. He worried with each train and boat he took. Finally, on September 4, 1838, Frederick Bailey reached New York City and began his life as a freeman.

3 ABOLITIONIST

In New York, slave catchers offered
people money for news about runaway
slaves. Even a black person might give
Frederick to the slave catchers. Frederick
was afraid to speak to anyone. At night, he
hid among the barrels on the harbor docks.

The next day, he finally risked speaking to a sailor. The sailor took him to the home of a man who helped runaway slaves. Frederick stayed there until Anna arrived in New York.

Frederick and Anna married and moved to New Bedford, Massachusetts, a seaport with many whaling ships. In New Bedford, Frederick changed his last name from Bailey to Douglass so slave catchers would not easily find him.

Anna and Frederick arrive in the whaling town of New Bedford.

Workers in New Bedford recaulk a whaling ship.

Frederick hoped to work as a caulker, sealing cracks in ships. But white caulkers did not want a black man working with them. So he sawed wood, swept chimneys, and dug cellars. Anna washed and ironed clothes for others. In 1839, they had a baby girl named Rosetta. In 1840, they had a son named Lewis.

In New Bedford, oxen were used instead of slaves. There was no sad singing, no loud swearing, and no whipping. Everyone owned books and read. People talked about the news of the day.

Frederick began reading the *Liberator*, a newspaper edited by William Lloyd Garrison. Garrison wanted to end slavery.

Frederick also went to antislavery meetings. In the summer of 1841, he went to a meeting in Nantucket. There, he was asked to speak about his life as a slave. Frederick stood trembling before the huge crowd. He felt as if he could hardly get out the words. When he finished, he couldn't remember what he had said. But the crowd cheered. They wanted Frederick to use his strong voice to speak out against slavery.

Frederick (RIGHT) attends an antislavery convention. It was a thrilling event.

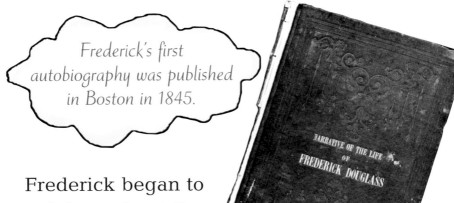

Frederick's first autobiography was published in Boston in 1845.

Frederick began to travel throughout the North. People paid him to speak about his life as a slave. When Frederick spoke, his words rang out as clear as a bell. His voice was deep, with thundering tones. People felt his speeches were like music.

Frederick kept reading and thinking about slavery. When he spoke, his words made people think. Soon he was speaking so well that people didn't believe he had been a slave. After all, a slave wouldn't have been educated.

To prove he was a slave, Frederick wrote his autobiography. He included the names of his slave masters. Now he was in great danger. Slave catchers would hunt for him.

Frederick left the country. His wife and children—Rosetta, Lewis, Frederick Jr., and Charles—stayed at home. He spoke to crowds all over Great Britain. He told them how slaves in America had "the initials of their master's name burned into their flesh." He asked the crowds to speak out against slavery.

His English friends raised money for him. Some of the money was used to buy Frederick's freedom. Frederick Douglass returned to America as a freeman. He moved his family to Rochester, New York. There he started a newspaper.

When Douglass spoke, he stood before crowds neatly dressed. Anna made sure his shirts were always sparkling white and neatly pressed.

Frederick's newspaper was called the *North Star*, after the star that had guided so many slaves to freedom. He wanted blacks to read. Then they would learn they had the right to be free. In the paper, Frederick printed news about antislavery speeches. He printed works by black writers.

Whites who read the paper were impressed. The paper was well written, with no grammatical mistakes. Frederick was showing the world that black people were just as smart as white people.

FREDERICK'S HELPERS

The office of the *North Star* was one room. Frederick's children helped set the letters for the printing press. Lewis and Charles folded and delivered the newspapers. But Anna never learned to read, so she could not fully share in Frederick's work. Yet she cooked a special meal to celebrate each new issue of the paper.

THUNDEROUS
4 WORDS
OF TRUTH

Since Frederick Douglass's newspaper brought in little money, he continued to give speeches. In July 1848, he spoke at the first women's rights meeting. Douglass believed that women should have the same rights as men. But for him slaves' rights would have to come first.

After the Fugitive Slave Act passed, slaves could be captured in free states, where before they had been safe. These slaves were caught in Boston, Massachusetts.

In 1850, Congress passed the Fugitive Slave Act. Now there was a *law* letting slave catchers drag runaway slaves back to the South. Anyone hiding a runaway slave could be put into prison.

The law frightened Douglass. He had bought his freedom. But could he still be taken by slave catchers? And what about the runaway slaves who had not bought their freedom? The only safe place for them was Canada, where slavery was illegal.

Douglass hid runaway slaves in his home. He fed them and raised money for their train tickets. He helped them board trains to Canada.

In 1852, he was asked to speak for the Independence Day celebration in Rochester, New York. But how could he speak on the holiday that honored American freedom? All Americans were not free—many were slaves.

PACKED THEATERS

In the 1800s, there were no movie theaters or televisions. But Americans often gathered in theaters for entertaining and educational events. People came to see plays, song-and-dance acts, and to hear lectures. Popular speakers toured the country and became famous. Crowds loved humorous speakers. But many people came to hear people like Frederick Douglass speak about important topics of the times.

Wherever he went, Douglass spoke with great power and passion.

But Douglass still had something to say. On July 5, he gave a fiery speech. His booming voice carried the words of truth. "Your sounds of rejoicing are empty and heartless," he said. He sounded a battle cry to shake up the nation and end slavery at once. "We need the storm, the whirlwind, and the earthquake."

In 1854, the Kansas-Nebraska Act opened western land to slavery. Douglass was furious. Slavery should not spread. Slavery should end!

One angry white man, John Brown, came to Douglass with a plan. Brown wanted groups of armed men to help slaves escape from their masters.

Douglass liked the idea of helping slaves. But then in October 1859, Brown changed his plans. He wanted to attack Harper's Ferry, West Virginia. The government stored guns there. Brown wanted to use the guns to start a slave revolt, and he wanted Douglass to join him.

John Brown led the raid on Harper's Ferry in his effort to end slavery.

Douglass was against the idea. It would be an attack on the government. He was sure Brown would fail. And he was right. Soldiers captured Brown and his men. They seized all of Brown's important papers.

Douglass was afraid he would be arrested. He had written letters to Brown. He had given Brown money. Would those letters be found? Would people think Douglass helped plan the attack?

Fearing the worst, Douglass fled to England. A few months later, his daughter Annie died. When he heard the news, he rushed home.

5 WINNING THE WAR

In March 1861, Abraham Lincoln became president. In April the Civil War began. Southerners wanted their independence from Northern states. Northerners wanted all states to remain united. Douglass and many others around the country saw slavery as the main cause of the war.

President Abraham Lincoln admired Frederick Douglass.

Douglass wanted blacks to join the Union Army. But many Northern whites, including Lincoln, did not want blacks in the army. They said that black soldiers would hurt the pride and spirit of white soldiers. They said that black soldiers would not be brave on the battlefield.

Douglass spoke against Lincoln. Lincoln must let blacks join the army, Douglass said. The Union Army needed black men to win the war.

By 1863, Lincoln saw that Douglass was right. But black men who joined the army were used to dig trenches. They were not treated as soldiers.

Douglass was saddened by the poor treatment of black men. But he still wanted them to fight. The United States was their country. As soldiers, blacks would show they deserved to be treated as citizens.

Douglass wrote an address to black men in the North. "Liberty won by white men would lose half its luster. . . . Better even die free, than to live slaves."

In the spring of 1863, Douglass toured New York, getting young black men to join the army as soldiers. His sons Charles and Lewis were the first in New York to enlist.

About 180,000 black soldiers served in the Union Army during the Civil War.

Black soldiers quickly showed their bravery. Many were wounded and killed in battles. Some were captured by the Confederate Army. They were beaten, killed, or sold into slavery. Hearing this, Douglass was outraged. He asked to speak with Lincoln.

Douglass went to the White House in August 1863. President Lincoln looked tired and worried. But as soon as he saw Douglass, his face lit up.

A black regiment attacks Fort Wagner, South Carolina, in 1863. Douglass's son Lewis fought in the battle.

Frederick wanted black soldiers to become officers like white soldiers. They should be leaders, too.

Lincoln listened carefully as Douglass spoke. Douglass wanted black soldiers to be treated fairly— and to get the same pay as white soldiers. Lincoln said being a soldier was an honor. Someday, blacks would get the same pay. But it wouldn't happen right away.

Black soldiers did brave deeds on the battlefields. Douglass wanted them to receive honors and become officers. Lincoln agreed. But he could not promise Douglass that this would be done. Douglass was not happy with all of Lincoln's remarks. But he liked Lincoln's honesty. Douglass helped get more blacks to join the army.

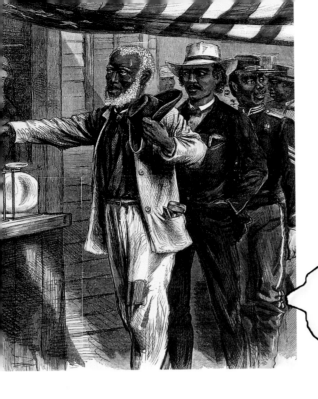

Black citizens vote for the first time.

In 1865, the Civil War ended. The North defeated the South. A few months later, Lincoln was killed. The country was shocked, and Douglass was deeply saddened. They had lost a great leader.

Later that year, all the slaves were freed. But they did not get full rights as citizens. Blacks needed jobs and the right to vote.

Douglass traveled in the North, speaking about blacks' right to vote. He went to the White House and spoke to President Andrew Johnson.

Douglass also wanted to see blacks get important government jobs. In 1872, at the age of fifty-four, Douglass moved his family to Washington, D.C. There, he was closer to the important jobs. In 1877, he became U.S. marshal for the District of Columbia. In 1881, he became recorder of deeds for the district.

In 1882, Douglass mourned when his wife, Anna, died. Then, seventeen months later, he shocked the country by marrying a white woman, Helen Pitts.

CEDAR HILL

In 1878, Douglass bought a fifteen-acre estate that overlooked Washington, D.C. Cedar trees surrounded the twenty-room house, so Douglass called his home Cedar Hill. The original owner of the estate hadn't wanted a black person ever to own the property. Cedar Hill is now a National Historic Site and is open to the public.

Blacks were angry. Why didn't Douglass marry a fine black woman? they asked. Wasn't a black woman good enough for him? Even Douglass's children were not happy with the marriage. Whites were upset too. But Douglass did not think that race should keep people apart. He and Helen loved each other. They shared the same interests. They were happy together.

Frederick sits with his wife Helen. Her sister Eva stands behind.

In 1889, Frederick became the United States minister to Haiti. He and Helen sailed there in October. Douglass helped with business deals between the United States and Haiti for the next two years.

On February 20, 1895, Douglass spent the afternoon at a meeting of the Women's Council. Later that day, he returned home and told Helen about the meeting. While he was speaking, Douglass fell to his knees and died.

Douglass was not afraid to die. He had faith in God, and he knew he had lived a good life. He had used his talents as a speaker and writer to make his country a better place. He had helped free the slaves. And he had helped free all Americans— black and white—from the evils of slavery.

TIMELINE

FREDERICK DOUGLASS
WAS BORN IN
FEBRUARY 1818.

In the year . . .

1824	Frederick's grandmother, Betsy Bailey, took him to the Lloyd plantation.	Age 6
1826	he was sent to Baltimore to work for Hugh Auld. he began to learn to read.	Age 8
1831	he bought *The Columbian Orator.*	Age 13
1833	he was sent to work for Thomas Auld, his master.	
1834	he was sent to work for Edward Covey.	Age 16
1835	he was sent to work for William Freeland.	
1836	he was sent back to Baltimore.	
1837	he met Anna Murray.	
1838	he escaped to New York City. he married Anna Murray. they moved to New Bedford, Massachusetts. he changed his last name to Douglass.	Age 20
1841	he attended the Anti-Slavery Society convention on Nantucket.	Age 23
1845	he wrote *Narrative of the Life of Frederick Douglass, an American Slave.*	Age 27
1847	he started a weekly newspaper, *The North Star.*	
1855	he wrote *My Bondage and My Freedom.*	Age 37
1872	he moved his family to Washington, D.C.	
1881	he wrote *The Life and Times of Frederick Douglass.*	Age 63
1882	his wife, Anna, died.	
1884	he married Helen Pitts, a white woman.	
1895	he died on February 20.	Age 77

FREDERICK'S VIOLIN

Frederick loved to play the violin. He probably learned to play when he was working in Baltimore as a young man. Anna encouraged his playing, and he became a fine musician, playing music by Handel, Haydn, and Mozart. You can see his violin at Cedar Hill.

Frederick's grandson Joseph (RIGHT) also became a violinist. When Joseph was a boy, he and his grandfather played Shubert together. Joseph became a professional violinist and performed on concert stages in cities like New York and Chicago. His grandfather was very proud of him.

FURTHER READING

NONFICTION

McKissack, Patricia C., and Fredrick L. McKissack. *Black Hands, White Sails: The Story of African-American Whalers.* New York: Scholastic, 1999. Recounts the stories of the black freemen and runaway slaves who sailed whaling ships in New England between 1730 and 1880.

McKissack, Patricia C., and Fredrick L. McKissack. *Rebels Against Slavery.* New York: Scholastic, 1996. The stories of the men and women who led slave revolts, including Cinque, Nat Turner, and John Brown.

Moore, Cathy. *The Daring Escape of Ellen Craft.* Minneapolis: Carolrhoda Books, 2002. Recounts the true story of Ellen and William Craft's escape from slavery.

Streissguth, Tom. *John Brown.* Minneapolis: Carolrhoda Books, 1999. The life of the abolitionist who led the raid on Harper's Ferry.

FICTION

McKissack, Patricia C., and Fredrick L. McKissack. *Christmas in the Big House, Christmas in the Quarters.* New York: Scholastic, 1994. The story of Christmas celebrations of both the slaveholding family and the slaves on a Virginia plantation in 1859.

Miller, William. *Frederick Douglass: The Last Day of Slavery.* New York: Lee & Low, 1996. A picture book about the day Frederick stood up to an overseer and fought back.

Rappaport, Doreen. *A Freedom River.* New York: Jump at the Sun, 2000. The dramatic story of an ex-slave, John Parker, who led hundreds of slaves to freedom on the Underground Railroad.

WEBSITES

American Visionaries: Frederick Douglass
www.cr.nps.gov/museum/exhibits/douglass/ This website
features items owned by Frederick Douglass.

Frederick Douglass National Historic Site
www.nps.gov/frdo/freddoug.html This website includes a
virtual tour of Cedar Hill and links to related sites.

Western New York Suffragists: Frederick Douglass
winningthevote.org/FDouglass.html A short biography of
Douglass, with links to people and events in his life.

SELECT BIBLIOGRAPHY

Blassingame, John W. *Frederick Douglas: The Clarion
    Voice.* Washington, DC: National Park Service, 1976.

Douglass, Frederick. *Life and Times of Frederick Douglass.*
    1892. Reprint, New York: Macmillan, 1962.

Douglass, Frederick. *My Bondage and My Freedom.* 1855.
    Reprint, New York: Crowell Publishing, 1966.

Douglass, Frederick. *Narrative of the Life of Frederick
    Douglass, an American Slave.* 1845. Reprint, New York:
    Dorer Publications, 1995.

Foner, Philip S., ed. *Frederick Douglass on Women's Rights.*
    New York: Da Capo Press, 1992.

McFeely, William S. *Frederick Douglass.* New York:
    W. W. Norton, 1991.

Quarles, Benjamin. *Frederick Douglass.* New York:
    Da Capo Press, 1997.

INDEX

Acknowledgments

For photographs and artwork: Library of Congress, pp. 4 (LC-USZ62-120533), 14 (LC-USZC2-1871), 21 (LC-USZ62-7823), courtesy of the Maryland State Archives, Special Collections (SC564-1-94), p. 7; © North Wind Picture Archives, pp. 8, 10, 18, 24, 30, 32, 36, 38, 40; Documenting the American South (http://docsouth.unc.edu), The University of North Carolina at Chapel Hill Libraries, from *Narrative of the Life and Times of Frederick Douglass, an American Slave, Written by Himself,* Boston, 1845, pp. 11, 13, 19, 23; © Hulton/Archive Photos, pp. 15, 39; Atkins Library Special Collection, University of North Carolina, Charlotte, p. 26; National Park Service, pp. 27, 42; Louisiana State Museum, p. 16; © Corbis, pp. 17, 45; Madison County Historical Society, Oneida, New York, p. 25; National Archives, pp. 33 (W&C115), 37 (W&C155). Front cover: National Archives (NWDNS-FL-FL-22). Back cover: Atkins Library—Special Collection, University of North Carolina, Charlotte.
For quoted material: pp. 11, 16, 27, 32, 37, Frederick Douglass, *Autobiographies: Narrative of the Life of Frederick Douglass, an American Slave; My Bondage and My Freedom; Life and Times of Frederick Douglass* (New York: Library of America, 1994).